AQUARIUS

A 28 Day Journey

By Tristiny Bell

First edition. September 2021.

Copyright © 2021 Tristiny Bell.

Written by Tristiny Bell.

Edited by Dr. S C. Lewis

Tristiny Bell
ISBN 978-0-578-98506-0

For the amazing Imogene Tina Crawford, I'd give my all.

For the woman who taught me everything from expressing my creativity to being the best young lady I can be.

For the Aquarius woman that could steal a room's attention without effort.

For you, I will always remember.

Rest Peacefully, my angel.

The Experience

This book is the product of a month-long journey. During the month of February 2019, I created a complete solitude environment and eliminated all distractions to embrace my creativity. Each day, no matter what happened or what I did, I had to write a poem. Each piece is not always about what occurred that day. Some pieces are past reflections, future goals, overall self-evaluations, or even just metaphoric jokes. Even with time passed, I experience each poem as if it was new

Join me as we experience Aquarius in all of its love, pain, happiness, fears, and honesty.

Day 1- Soon

It's like I'm living a lie.
When I know I'm not who I want to be
Or should be.

I'm lying to myself.

This isn't you
But this is what you have to do
Who you have to be
How do I combine both worlds?
Where I'm free and able.
I desire to live in my truth
I need to live in my truth
I just don't quite know how
Yet
But soon!

Day 2- Hangover

Aches and throbs
I knew better
Than to drown my feelings
But this whiskey hitting different

Just moving and living
Still with no vision
As long as I'm breathing
Damn this whiskey hitting different

Slow walks; deep breaths
Trying not to forget
Last night- what a trip
Just something about this whiskey

The sun rises; but I fall
Calling out. Can't move.
I'll try again tomorrow
Now it's back to me and this whiskey

Day 3 - 4:55am

Today I thought of you
The old you— the old us
Never official but always love
Your intimacy is craved

La lengua— can't forget your talk
When it moves, wisdom flows
Vibes pour out and I come closer
Closer and closer and closer

Blunt but true—
I almost fell in love with you
Almost but for sure deep lust
Our shadows unveiled even at 1pm

Can you hold me like you used to?
Just so I can smell you
A lingering scent I've tried to forget
You were so full of shit; yet heaven sent

Day 4 - A Different Day

Woke up feeling different
A happy different
That happy different after
you done had a few
That happy different when
You're on a spiritual high
That happy different when
You just don't know why
But you feel a different happy
Maybe not even happy
But content
At peace even
Free
You just feel able.
Able to do, think, or feel.
Without worries or criticism
Because you are fluid
"You" is fluid
Your todays are not your tomorrows
So today You...
better be happy for today

Day 5 – Skip

This one will be short.
One eye open
Fetal position
Stomach churning knots
Debating on medicine
Another day I'll bring them charm
But right now.....

Day 6- Happy Birthday My Angel

One minute you're here
Then you're gone the next
Death is such a weird concept
It's amazing how your entire world
Can crash in minutes
I see you often
In my dreams
Just as you were
It's weird
My dreams have tricked themselves
Believing you're a call away
Maybe you are
Because I feel your spirit
Around me
Near me
Even within me
Maybe you are here
As an angel dressed in disguise
Protecting and teaching
Keeping me from my ways
It's weird
I'll always remember
When I see you again
I got a funny story to tell you

Day 7- Happy Birthday My Angel Pt 2

Don't cry

Those words engraved.
You lay there calm, yet worried.
I think you knew.
A tear falls.
I stare into your eyes.
The background fades.
It's just me and you.
Squeezing your hand,
As if I was begging you to be ok.
I squeeze harder.
Another tear falls.
Pain comes over your face.
But you're still so calm.
I squeeze harder.
Another tear falls.
Please
Be ok
I saw in your face, you knew.
Then I knew.
.... and another tear falls
Where the fuck is the ambulance!?
I squeeze harder

You were slipping away
And there was nothing I could do
Nothing
The person I admire the most
Was slipping away before my eyes
I'm helpless
Worst pain I'll ever feel

Calmly and brave
Your last wish; your last words:

Don't cry.

But the tears kept falling.
I'm sorry. I failed.

No matter how hard I try.
Even until this day
At every memory,
I cry

Tall
Well taller than me
And that's not hard to beat
Dark
And handsome

Of course, the basics
But let's dig a little deeper

A beautiful soul whose actions
stand behind just that

A touch,
a touch to make my spirit flutter with peace

Strength to weather any storm

Can you be my umbrella?
Can you rid a path of obstacles?
Can you find God in a room of evil?
Can correct your bad habits?

Because that's my IBM.

Day 9 - Lace Up

Step away sometimes
Or run
Run away from the negative
Not every battle is yours to fight

But right now,
I'm running and fighting
At the same time
I want to give up
But I can't
I can't
I've come too far

I want to stop running.
My feet are killing me
My shoes are wearing out

So, do I switch to sneakers?
Do I change lanes?
Because my feet are killing me.

Maybe I should just keep on
Running and fighting.
A swing with each step

Something will give sooner or later.
But I can't keep on like this forever,
I got asthma.

Day 10- Tired

Being tired is exhausting
Life is just tiring
Rather you're doing too much
Or not doing enough

You're still tired?
You'll rest when you're dead, right?
But what about now?
I'm tired now

Day 11- Home

Familiar faces
Good vibes
Crazy laughs
Memories flowing
This feels like home
Comfortable place
Food plates
Warm hugs
Good to be home
Happy tears
Wishful thoughts
Soft prayers
Giant smiles
I'm finally home

Day 12- Secret

Out of all my secrets, you're my fav
We can blend during the day
And play all night
They'll never know it.
In plain sight
And still unseen
You're my favorite secret
And if I could tell anyone,
I'd still tell you
Because we're best friends but
Mr. Jones, we gotta thing going on

Day 13- Ms. Forecast

The longer the hair
The thicker the head
Filled with knowledge
Down to the dread

Chocolate completion
She's damn near perfect
Skin like clouds
Body meaner than storms
You can see the sun in her eyes
Like it never rains in southern Californ—

Yea you get the picture
Dripping in the rain
You can swim in her river
Baby like the weather
Can't predict her every move
Make you wanna stay outside
Now, let me tell you 'bout her moon
It's an eclipse tonight

Day 14- Talk to Me

The power in silence consumes us.
We inhale it like a deep breath
Right before the perfect mistake.
A single breath.
Silently loud
I hear you say everything
When your mouth is closed.
Locked even
But there's silence in your talk
Our bodies speak
Then we breathe

Damn I love this conversation

Day 15- Anxiety

I try to stay calm
The worry never stops
Try after try
Then it's overthought thoughts
On what hasn't even occurred
Gotta plan for the worst
Can't shake this feeling
About what could happen
Still carrying on panic
Fingers just tappin'
Eyes closed mind shut
Exhale to relax
A second at a time
To bring reality back

Day 16- Checkmate

Too proud for love
But you're the one I trust.
That's past tense
Cause I'm pass this
See with me. Falling in is hard.
But jumping out is easy
I just might hurt ya
More than you thought you did me
Not to brag or to boast
Playing me is like playing yourself
Because the old me really never left

Day 17- Jermaine Flow

I've typed then erased
Can't find the right words to say
My mind is trippin
Not knowing what to say
But don't know how
Not overwhelmed just restless
Ima let this Allstar ride.
I'll start, He'll finish the rest

Day 18- Set the Mood

Let the lights flicker
Switching colors
Changing temperature
Relax and unwind
Just take a seat
Open your mind
The moment is for the now
No time for the past
I'll let you watch
Just as long as you ask
My favorite scent lingers
As the room gets dimmer
It can get a lil uncomfortable
But tonight, just relax

Day 19- Dedication

The easy way out
Can be the hardest road
I'm measuring twice
Because when I cut,
I'm slicing
My journey isn't perfect
But it's worth it
So, when I get all I deserve
You're going to feel this story

I could be just talking
But baby just wait
Watch my actions
Match the vibe in my words
I'll have your pulse shake

I could be just talking
But I'm tryna be the reason you
Pulling old tricks like a rabbit
Turn loving to a habit
Put those arms to use
And make 'em pick up the groove

I could be just talking
Because that smile got me lost
Time traveling til infinity like its '93
And there's a lil mischief in my soul
But I ain't tryna hear no
So, baby say it slow

I could be just talking
Saying all the right things
To get you right where I want you
And that's where you should be
Standing close, near, right beside me

I could be just talking
So listen very close
I'm the master of disguise
But this ain't no joke
I wanna make you laugh
Or make you believe

I could be just talking
But baby you ain't heard a thing

Day 21- My God

Can I tell you a little about my God
My, he works in mysterious ways
It almost makes you laugh
Have you feeling hopeless
But if you remain patient
You have all you prayed

Our relationship hasn't been perfect
But he's always there
Even when I don't deserve it
Don't get caught in a name.
So, if you believe just believe
Be aware of any Man that doesn't
He has nothing to fear
And nothing to lose
To each is own
But I know the truth

Day 22- Frenemy

Cold blooded
The way you disrespect my mind
And torture my soul

We've known each other for years
You visit every few months
Sometimes you stay longer
But only when times get rough

I wish we never met
But at times I don't regret
Because you taught me many lessons
I guess meeting you was a blessing

I cried nights because of you
Even when you had a strong hold
I couldn't ever just let go

When you're here, I'm not
My spirit takes a vacation
Until you leave, then I'm back

Right now, I'm great.
And I found my secret weapon
For your next visitation.

Dancing in the flames
Feeling the heat
Unbothered by the colors
Just moving to the beat

My lungs full of smoke
The smog gets thicker
I ignore all signs
Even if my body gets weaker

It's all fun, right?
But shit going left
Digging a deeper hole
If I take one more step

Day 24- Rain

Drip

Drip

It starts off slow

Then louder and louder

Beating my window

These days are bittersweet

You clean you cook

You work on "me"

Catch up on rest

And relax your feet

Rain

Rain

I can't stand it

Ann was right

Sweet memories came quick

Can't ponder right now

It's time to do shit

Day 25 - Have You Met Her?

You mind if I get a little deep?
I just wanna introduce you
To the real me
See you may not know her
She's something like a secret
Like a soft whisper
But will get loud
If ya mistreat her
A prize I'd say the least
Her soul makes your heart
Skip beats
In tuned, bold, and brave
It's genuine and rare
Just gotta get pass
That hard shell phase

Tough as nails
But dig a little further
And you find the core
The squishy gentle center
I swear it's love in the middle
She got bark and bite
With true pain behind
those strong brown eyes
A fighter til she dies
But she knows when to quit
You gotta meet this chick
Well women— young lady
Sure enough
She'll drive ya crazy

But the ride is beautiful
And somewhat poetic.

Are you down for the ride?
One you'll never forget
Swear you won't forget it

Day 26- It's Almost Perfect

It can't be faked
The realness in your eyes
Can be felt
You can taste the happiness
As pure joy slides
Down your throat
But it's also pain
Crippling but bearable
Beautiful daggers
Never felt so good
Then there's endurance
It's like moving mountains through a storm
Yet you keep fighting every round
Blow by blow
Rolling with the punches
But it's also intimate
Seductive eyes and kind whispers
Feels like Christmas morning
The angel without the snow
It's almost perfect
Almost

Day 27- A Bad Dream

My strengths have become my weaknesses

After years of suppression
I've become numb
Numb to things
That use to be fun
Happy and joy
Yet I feel nothing
I blame the pain
Pain and depress
Still can't express
Cause of damn suppress
But I'm strong
Too strong to where I'm damaged
Yea I swear I can handle it
And I can
But it hurts
It hurts deep inside
Yet I hide
With a smile
And grin
I laugh but within
Its tears
To fill a lake
Wait- that strength
Ohhh comes pouring in
Then I feel - nothing
I shake it off
And keep going
Because I gotta prepare
For the next one.
They say storms come in 3's
But mine is never-ending

Then I wake
From a terrible dream
Right before I get happy
I realize it's reality
Then I repeat

Day 28- Alonely

To be lonely is
To long for the company of others
To feel saddened without it
It's an unsettling feeling
You are not satisfied

To be alone is
To be content with your own company
It's pleasing to be by yourself
It's a relaxing feeling
You are at peace

These days...
My mind is alone
But my heart is lonely
It's crazy. The love
I used to feel
The feeling I used to know
And my mind
It's calmed
Where's the compromise,
The middle ground?
Alone days
And lonely nights